I0759745

Gaten Matarazzo

Kurt Waldendorf

childsworld.com

Published by The Child's World®
800-599-READ • www.childsworld.com

Copyright © 2026 by The Child's World®
All rights reserved. No part of this book may be reproduced or utilized in any form or by any means without written permission from the publisher.

Photography Credits
Photographs ©: Evan Agostini/Invision/AP Images, cover, 1; Kathy Hutchins/Shutterstock Images, 5, 16; 21 Laps Ent/Monkey Massacre/Album/Alamy, 7; Shutterstock Images, 9, 10, 21, 23, 25; Kostas Lymperopoulos/Cal Sport Media/AP Images, 13; Walter McBride/WireImage/Getty Images, 15; Wikimedia Commons, 19; Bruce Glikas/Getty Images Entertainment/Getty Images, 27; Theo Wargo/Getty Images for Tony Awards Productions/Getty Images Entertainment/Getty Images, 28; Design elements from Shutterstock Images

ISBN Information
9781503875708 (Reinforced Library Binding)
9781503876675 (Portable Document Format)
9781503877177 (Online Multi-user eBook)
9781503877795 (Electronic Publication)

LCCN 2025938203

Printed in the United States of America

ABOUT THE AUTHOR

Kurt Waldendorf is the author of more than a dozen books for children. When he's not writing or editing, he enjoys indoor rock climbing and running along the shores of Lake Michigan with his dog. He lives in Chicago.

TABLE of CONTENTS

CHAPTER ONE

Getting the Part

Gaten Matarazzo looked into the video camera. The 12-year-old actor introduced himself. His voice was cheerful. But, a moment later, Gaten's face changed. His voice became serious, and he began to speak his lines.

It was an important moment for Gaten. He was recording an **audition** for a new TV show. The show would become known as *Stranger Things*. Gaten was trying out for the role of Mike Wheeler, the main character.

Gaten Matarazzo had no idea when auditioning for *Stranger Things* that it would eventually win Best Show at the 2018 MTV Movie and TV Awards.

Gaten's audition video showed off his personality. It also showed his way of speaking. Gaten had a **lisp** caused by a condition called cleidocranial dysplasia (CCD). CCD affects the way people's bones and teeth grow. For Gaten, it meant he was born without collarbones. He also needed surgeries to remove extra teeth that grew in. He had missed out on roles because of CCD in the past. He hoped this audition would be different.

SURPRISE AUDITION

Gaten's *Stranger Things* audition took him by surprise. He had done two other auditions that week. He had forgotten about *Stranger Things* until his mom woke him up to go to the audition. Gaten studied his lines in the car on the way to the studio. Afterward, he thought the audition was the worst of his life. He was shocked when he got a **callback** for the part.

Dustin Henderson (middle) is a favorite character among *Stranger Things* fans. Gaten's humor comes through in the role.

The show's **producers**, Matt and Ross Duffer, watched Gaten's video. They watched it only one time, but it was enough to make a decision. Gaten was not right for the role of Mike Wheeler. But his charming smile, cheerful attitude, and **authentic** personality made him perfect for another character. The Duffer brothers eventually offered Gaten the role of Dustin Henderson.

The decision paid off. The first season of *Stranger Things* was a hit. After it released in 2016, the show quickly became one of the biggest hits for the streaming platform Netflix. *Stranger Things* brought Gaten's career to a new level. He appeared in music videos, commercials, and movies. He spoke with talk-show hosts about CCD. He even got to host his own TV show. Before long, Gaten had become one of Hollywood's most popular young stars.

Gaten attended the 2017 American Music Awards. He helped announce a musical performance with some of his *Stranger Things* costars.

Gaten was born in New London, Connecticut (pictured). His family moved to New Jersey when he was about 2 months old.

CHAPTER TWO

Pursuing a Passion

Gaetano "Gaten" John Matarazzo III was born on September 8, 2002. His parents are Heather and Gaetano. Gaten has an older sister named Sabrina and a younger brother named Carmen. Gaten grew up with his family in Little Egg Harbor, New Jersey.

Shortly after he was born, Gaten was **diagnosed** with CCD. But he did not let CCD keep him from his interests. He began taking voice lessons at an early age. Sabrina was also a singer and actor. While she performed at a showcase in New York, she met a **manager** who signed her. Soon after, Sabrina's manager also asked if Gaten wanted to perform. Gaten responded yes, and decided to give acting a try, too.

When Gaten was 7 years old, he began auditioning for roles in musical theater. He had dreams of performing on Broadway. Broadway is New York City's theater district. It also refers more generally to the world of live theater. He faced a lot of rejections. Many had to do with the way he looked or spoke. The hardest rejection was for a role in *Les Misérables*. A production was touring in the United States. The musical was one of Gaten's favorites. He dreamed of playing Gavroche. But the casting director thought Gaten was too short for the part.

BROTHER-SISTER DUO

Sabrina Matarazzo is an actor and social media **influencer**. Sabrina and Gaten have performed together many times. The pair sang the national anthem at a New York Mets baseball game in 2015. In 2019, Sabrina and Gaten appeared with other family members on the game show *Family Feud*.

Gaten loved to sing growing up. In 2017, he sang the US national anthem at a National Hockey League game.

Gaten did not give up. He took dance lessons to improve his skills. He auditioned for roles up to three times per week. Still, after each audition, the answer was no. In 2011, Gaten tried something different. He entered a talent competition. He performed a vocal solo. Gaten made it all the way to the national competition. He took third place.

Following the competition, Gaten landed his first role. It was not just any role. It was a part in a Broadway musical called *Priscilla, Queen of the Desert*. After 2 years of rejections, Gaten had finally made it! But Broadway was hard work. In the morning, Gaten went to school in New Jersey. In the afternoon, he traveled 2 hours to New York City for **rehearsal**. He did his homework when he was not onstage. Gaten often got home after 1 a.m. Then he would wake up and do it again the next day.

Gaten's hard work paid off. In 2013, he tried out once more for *Les Misérables*. This time, he got the part. He joined the touring production as Gavroche. He was then cast in the 2014 Broadway production. The show was nominated for a Tony Award. This award is the highest honor in musical theater.

Gaten played Gavroche in *Les Misérables* from 2014 to 2015. The show was in New York City at the Imperial Theatre.

Gaten and his *Stranger Things* costars Caleb McLaughlin (center) and Millie Bobbie Brown (right) attended the Emmy Awards in 2016.

Gaten loved musical theater. But finding opportunities was hard. He began trying out for TV roles, too. In 2015, an upcoming show called *Montauk* caught Gaten's eye. The show was about a group of kids investigating strange and scary events in their town. It took place in Long Island, New York. Gaten liked the idea of filming close to his home in New Jersey. He accepted the role thinking he would appear in only a few episodes. But the role and the show became much bigger than he imagined. This is the show that would become *Stranger Things*.

CHAPTER THREE

Stranger Things Success

Gaten began acting for his new role in November 2015. By that time, many things about the show had changed. The title had been updated from *Montauk* to *Stranger Things*. The show was no longer set in New York. It now took place in the fictional city of Hawkins, Indiana. Much of the filming was done in Atlanta, Georgia.

Still, Gaten was excited for the opportunity. As the Duffer brothers got to know Gaten, his role grew. They wrote Gaten's CCD into the script. They added jokes he told his castmates. Gaten had become part of the main cast. This meant he would appear in every episode.

The first season of *Stranger Things* was mostly filmed in Atlanta, Georgia. A key location of the show was the Hawkins National Laboratory. The building used for this lab is owned by Emory University in Atlanta.

Four other actors were selected for the young group of friends on the show. They were Finn Wolfhard, Millie Bobby Brown, Caleb McLaughlin, and Noah Schnapp. The actors quickly became friends in real life. Gaten bonded with Finn over their love of movies. He connected with Caleb about working on Broadway.

Filming was hard work. The young actors attended school on set in the morning. They filmed in the afternoon and evening. In total, the cast spent more than 6 months on set. Gaten wondered if the show was worth so much time away from home. He wondered whether the show would continue after the first season.

WORK IN PROGRESS

Gaten had a lot going on in his career. But he continued to make time for his life at home. When he was not filming, he attended Pinelands High School in New Jersey. He was active in the school's theater group. Gaten also started a band with his brother and sister called Work in Progress. The band performed small gigs around their hometown.

Gaten and his costars (from left to right) Caleb, Finn, and Noah, attended the Los Angeles, California, premiere for season two of *Stranger Things* in 2017.

On July 15, 2016, the first season of *Stranger Things* was released. All eight episodes appeared on Netflix. It did not take long for feedback to come in. About 8.2 million people watched the show in its first 16 days. Just over a month after *Stranger Things* was first released, the show was renewed for a second season.

Gaten was used to being in the spotlight. But *Stranger Things* brought him a whole new level of attention. Fans talked about the show's actors on social media. Some people made fun of Gaten for his lisp. But most were supportive. People liked that he talked about his CCD in the show. They felt he was bringing important attention to the disorder.

The support inspired Gaten and his father to help start an organization called CCD Smiles. The group raises money for children with CCD. Surgical procedures for the disorder can be expensive. CCD Smiles helps people pay for surgeries. Gaten hoped this would help kids with CCD pursue their dreams.

The success of *Stranger Things* also allowed Gaten to try new things. He appeared with Finn, Caleb, and Noah on the reality TV show *Lip Sync Battle* in 2017. Later that year, he got a role in pop star Katy Perry's "Swish Swish" music video. And in 2018, *The Hollywood Reporter* named him one of Hollywood's top 30 stars under 30 years old.

Gaten's career took another step forward in 2019. He became the host of a hidden-camera show called *Prank Encounters*. The show put strangers into weird and sometimes scary situations. The show filmed their reactions. The role allowed Gaten to go off script. It highlighted his friendly and playful personality.

GATEN MATARAZZO'S STAR MOMENTS

Gaten Matarazzo has been involved in many shows and films as both a lead and minor character. These are some of his appearances.

2011

Priscilla, Queen of the Desert

2014

Les Misérables

2016–2025

Stranger Things

2019

The Angry Birds Movie 2

2022

Honor Society

2022

Dear Evan Hansen

2023

Sweeney Todd

2024

Lego Star Wars: Rebuild the Galaxy

CHAPTER FOUR

Delays and Dream Roles

The year 2020 brought big changes for Matarazzo. In January, he had surgery to remove 14 baby teeth. This would allow his adult teeth to grow in. And he was set to graduate from Pinelands High School in May. But 2020 also brought big changes for the world.

A few days into filming the fourth season of *Stranger Things*, the show was put on hold. The COVID-19 **pandemic** had spread. Some schools and businesses were shut down. People were supposed to stay home to keep from getting sick. The pandemic affected people around the world. It was not clear if or when the show would continue.

Gaten and his castmates went to the world premiere of season three of *Stranger Things* in Santa Monica, California.

The pandemic helped put things into perspective for Matarazzo. He was no longer around his friends every day on set. He got a job at a local restaurant. When *Stranger Things* started filming again 6 months later, Gaten had a new sense of purpose. He approached each day wanting to learn and grow.

Matarazzo began planning for life after *Stranger Things*. He was no longer a child actor. He was ready to take on different kinds of roles. In 2022, Matarazzo played a leading role in the film *Honor Society*, a romantic comedy. He also embraced voice acting. In 2024, he voiced Sig Greebling in a TV series called *Lego Star Wars: Rebuild the Galaxy*. As a longtime Star Wars fan, the part was a dream role for Matarazzo.

In 2022, Matarazzo played Jared Kleinman in *Dear Evan Hansen*. He took a picture with his family at the closing-night performance.

In 2023, Matarazzo (center) played Tobias Ragg in the musical *Sweeney Todd*.

Still, his heart was in musical theater. In 2023, Matarazzo earned a major role in the Broadway musical *Sweeney Todd*. The role was the most difficult of his career. The show ran for 7 months with seven shows per week. Matarazzo loved the challenge. He hoped to continue working on Broadway in the future.

In 2024, Matarazzo finished filming the fifth and final season of *Stranger Things*. While on set for the last episode, the cast celebrated Matarazzo's 22nd birthday. The group had worked on the show for almost a decade. They had all become like family.

Matarazzo knew he would probably never have an opportunity like *Stranger Things* again. He was grateful for the opportunities the show had given him. He was also happy for the friends he made along the way. Whatever comes next for Matarazzo, he plans to bring the same positive attitude that led to his first big breakthrough. And he hopes to continue inspiring others to do the same.

IN HIS WORDS

Gaten Matarazzo was a star on *Stranger Things*, but he is growing into his own person off the show, too. He says:

“*Stranger Things* will beyond very likely be the biggest thing I will ever do and will most likely be the thing that I am remembered for. . . . And I am so cool with that as long as it facilitates happiness going forward, security, and more work.”

Source: “Gaten Matarazzo: Stranger Things Growing Pains, Saying Goodbye to Dustin & His Dream Come True!” YouTube, uploaded by Inside of You with Michael Rosenbaum, May 28, 2024. www.youtube.com.

GLOSSARY

audition (aw-DIH-shun) An audition is a tryout for a role or part, often by singing or reading material. Gaten was cast in *Stranger Things* despite not being well prepared for his audition.

authentic (aw-THEN-tuk) A person who is authentic is true to their personality or character. Gaten's audition tape showed his authentic personality.

callback (CALL-bak) A callback is a second or additional audition. Gaten was surprised to get a callback after his first audition for *Stranger Things*.

diagnosed (dy-uhg-NOHSD) To be diagnosed is to recognize something as a disease or condition. Gaten was diagnosed with CCD when he was a child.

facilitates (fuh-SI-luh-tayts) Facilitates means to make something easier. Matarazzo said he was okay with being remembered for *Stranger Things* more than his other projects as long as it facilitates future work and happiness.

influencer (IN-floo-en-sir) An influencer is someone who creates interest in products by posting about them on social media. Gaten's sister, Sabrina, is a social media influencer.

lisp (LISP) A lisp is when a person cannot pronounce the letters S and Z in the usual ways. Gaten spoke with a lisp.

manager (MAN-ih-juhr) A manager is someone who conducts business for another person. Gaten's manager helped sign him up for auditions.

pandemic (pan-DEH-mik) A pandemic is an outbreak of a disease that spreads across many places. The COVID-19 pandemic shut down schools and businesses.

producers (pruh-DOO-sirz) Producers are people who supervise or pay for artistic projects. The producers loved Gaten's audition tape for *Stranger Things*.

rehearsal (ree-HER-sull) Rehearsal is practice, usually for a performance. For his first Broadway show, Gaten traveled 2 hours to New York City for rehearsal.

FAST FACTS

- ★ Gaetano "Gaten" John Matarazzo III was born on September 8, 2002. His parents are Heather and Gaetano.
- ★ Gaten has cleidocranial dysplasia (CCD). He started an organization called CCD Smiles to raise money for kids who need surgery for CCD.
- ★ After taking third place in a national talent competition, Gaten was selected for a Broadway show called *Priscilla, Queen of the Desert* (2011).
- ★ Gaten auditioned for the role of Mike Wheeler on *Stranger Things*. The producers offered him the part of Dustin Henderson. They wrote the character to fit his personality.

ONE STRIDE FURTHER

- ★ Matarazzo worked hard to get selected for roles. What do you think it took for him to keep trying and not give up?
- ★ What does it take to become a Broadway star? Create a list and have a friend do the same. Compare your lists.
- ★ What actor or artist do you find most inspiring? Write a paragraph describing the things that inspire you about them.
- ★ If you performed, would you prefer working in theater, television, or movies? Why?

FIND OUT MORE

IN THE LIBRARY

Gagne, Tammy. *Ariana Grande*. Parker, CO: The Child's World, 2026.

Williams, Heather DiLorenzo. *Center Stage with Millie Bobby Brown*. Fremont, CA: Full Tilt Press, 2021.

Yacka, Douglass, and Francesco Sedita. *Where Is Broadway?* New York City, NY: Penguin Random House, 2019.

ON THE WEB

Visit our website for links about Gaten Matarazzo:

childsworld.com/links

Note to Parents, Caregivers, Teachers, and Librarians: We routinely verify our web links to make sure they are safe and active sites. So encourage your readers to check them out!

INDEX